Bibliographic information published by the German National Library:

The German National Library lists this publication in the National Bibliography; detailed bibliographic data are available on the Internet at http://dnb.dnb.de .

Imprint:

Copyright © 2017 GRIN Verlag
Print and binding: Books on Demand GmbH, Norderstedt Germany
ISBN: 9783668660403

This book at GRIN:

https://www.grin.com/document/413003

Abdallah Ziraba, Mbata David

Forecasting Cloud Storage Consumption Using Regression Model

GRIN Verlag

GRIN - Your knowledge has value

Since its foundation in 1998, GRIN has specialized in publishing academic texts by students, college teachers and other academics as e-book and printed book. The website www.grin.com is an ideal platform for presenting term papers, final papers, scientific essays, dissertations and specialist books.

Visit us on the internet:

http://www.grin.com/

http://www.facebook.com/grincom

http://www.twitter.com/grin_com

FORECASTING CLOUD STORAGE CONSUMPTION USING REGRESSION MODEL.

Authors:

1) *Abdallah Ziraba, lecturer ICT Department. The ICT University Yaounde Cameroon*
2) *Mbata David, Scholar and Researcher. ICT Department. The ICT University Yaounde Cameroon*

Abstract

The primary aim of the study was to develop a regression model for forecasting monthly cloud storage consumption. Second, to ascertain if the month is a reliable predictor of cloud storage capacity consumed. The model was developed using Minitab18 statistical software. The dependent variable was cloud storage capacity consumed, while the independent variable was the month of cloud storage consumption. The model was validated by checking the assumptions of regression to establish its suitability in making future predictions. Twelve-month data sets was analyzed to make future prediction for each passing month. The model made predictions with near accuracy from the actual cloud storage data consumed in each month. The model determines the intervals of monthly storage consumption. The study concluded that the month is a globally significant linear predictor of cloud storage capacity consumed over a period.

Key words: Cloud computing, forecasting model, storage capacity

Table of Contents

1.0. Introduction

Cloud computing is the most rapidly growing field of Information Technology (IT) and has been adopted by many organization for better IT infrastructure. Cloud computing platforms provide easy access to a company's high-performance computing and storage infrastructure through the cloud provider's web services. According to (Harvey, 2017), the cloud platforms are relatively cheaper than dedicated infrastructure for storage. Cloud storage offers high scalability with nearly 100 percent reliability, and high performance.

Consequently, many business activities are being performed through cloud computing. The cloud storage cost is based on the metered capacity consumed. Based on service consumption and business needs, organizations are billed in gigabyte (GB) per month. This means that organizations need to forecast their storage consumption to enable the potential IT managers to budget ahead. Cloud storage forecasting model becomes important as we are in the era of internet of things (IoT) when (McKendrick, 2016) said that much data will be generated. The model is rather more important as we near the predicted year for internet of everything (IoE). Cloud Infrastructure as a Service (IaaS) will be much in demand for data storage.

Therefore, the researchers have considered forecasting cloud storage consumption using regression model as a remedy for determining interval of cloud storage consumption for the organizations. Forecasting cloud storage usage based historic data has the potential to guide IT managers in effective budgeting and information system auditing.

Background of the study

Forecasting cloud storage consumption based on historical data can serve as a valuable source of guidance in IT budgeting and effective decision-making. According to (Chandini, Pushpalatha, and Ramesh, 2016), regression as a statistical modelling technique is very helpful for the future event forecasting based on timely and reliable figures. (Yanshuang, Na, Hong, and Yongqiang , 2015), submitted that regression model is an effective tool for investigating the relationship between two or more variables, and its purpose is to predict the change of response variable with respect to changes of decision variables.

The regression model predicts cloud infrastructure performance and even availability of cloud network resource like availability of servers. Similarly, the regression model predicts cloud storage capacity consumed in megabyte (MB) or GB, with high precision and near accuracy especially, for large series of data. The model gives ranges of cloud storage consumed over each passing month or a period, which can guide decision making in an organization.

Problem statement

Earlier (Kondo, 2009) asserted that the cost-benefits of cloud computing compared to traditional IT infrastructure and what constitutes the cost of cloud computing ranging from computational size, time, and storage is not perfectly clear to some organization and their IT managers. (Linthicum, 2014), affirmed that dynamic workloads and changing prices of cloud computing, most enterprises seem to be getting worse at understanding their storage actual storage cost.

(McKendrick, 2016), stated that in the coming years, one of the major forces driving cloud storage services in the organizations will be Internet of Things (IoT) and associated big data. The report says the ugly implications of this evolution is that organizations do not have enough storage capacity to handle the terabytes of data that will be generated. Therefore, nearly all workload will be cloud-borne and organization will contract storage services. Recently (RightScale, 2017), reaffirmed this problem through its conducted annual state of the cloud survey, which shows that understanding cloud storage service consumption and managing cloud costs has become a top challenge to companies. Consequently, the researchers developed a regression-forecasting model, for prediction of the future cloud storage consumption based on historical data. Without this forecasting model, organizations will find it difficult to determine the ranges of their cloud storage consumption and budget accordingly.

Objectives of the study:

The first objective of the study was to develop a new forecasting model for predicting cloud storage consumption in the organization. Second, to find out if the month is a good predictor of cloud storage capacity consumption.

Research hypothesis:

HO: $\beta1 = 0$ (Change in cloud storage capacity consumed does not depend on the change in the month of consumption).

HA: $\beta1 \neq 0$ (Change in storage capacity consumed depends on the change in the month of consumption).

Decision Rule: Reject H0, for probability value (p-value) < alpha (α) = 0.05 (5%) level of significance.

2.0. Related works/ Review of related literature

Many studies have reported different models for forecasting cloud computing. (Yanshuang, Na, Hong, and Yongqiang , 2015), predicted energy consumption in cloud data center using about four different regression models (nonlinear, linear, support vector, polynomial and exponential regression models). The models performances was investigated; it was concluded that all kinds of linear models had similar prediction performance, and therefore was good to model energy consumption with linear models for the performance counters. It was based on this recorded success of regression models in predicting energy consumption in cloud data center that it becomes only logical for the researchers to investigate the performance of linear regression model in predicting cloud data storage consumption.

(Baughman, McAvoy, McCrory, and O'Connell, 2016), developed a forecasting model for cloud server provisioning. The model was developed using Java programming. With the model, servers are independently provisioned based upon the forecast demand output. The model determines how many cloud resources to provision or de-provision. From the model, P (t) represents the number of servers to provision at the time, while the total capacity of the server is represented by βc. It was concluded that the model could forecast many servers availability for future workloads using IBM as a case study. This model though reported perfect for server availability forecasting but not suitable for predicting cloud storage consumption over the month. This is simply because the server-provisioning model cannot determine the intervals of monthly cloud storage consumption.

Similarly, (Lu, Panneerselvam, Liu and Wu, 2016), reported the success of a workload forecasting model for smart cloud computing. The model was based on Neuron model and was developed using MATLAB. The model is an answer to the cloud computing smart prediction of workload. It has a high precision, reliability and prediction accuracy of workload characteristics. Against the recorded success of this model in forecasting workload, it will fail in predicting ranges of cloud storage consumption over the month. (Vazquez, Krishnan, and John, 2016), studied cloud data center workloads for dynamic resource provisioning using time series model which defers from regression model. As the researcher is not interested in investigating trend.

(Chandini, Pushpalatha, and Ramesh, 2016), also investigated cloud server load prediction using three different methods; the Bayesian model, Prediction Based on Phase Space Reconstruction (PSR) method and the Group Method of Data Handling (GMDH) based on Evolutionary Algorithm(EA), Support vector and kalmann smoother based on Support Vector Regression and Neural Network Load Prediction. Against the recorded success of these models in forecasting workload, it also fails in predicting the ranges of cloud storage capacity consumed overs a period.

(Khan, 2016), developed a model for cloud data center load forecasting using dependent mixture model based on Bayesian inference. The model was aimed at predicting the unforeseen day-ahead cloud data center load. The efficiency of the model in scheduling and operating a cloud data center was reported. However, the model is has no history of efficiency in forecasting cloud storage capacity consumed with intervals of monthly consumption.

Obviously, all existing models have failed to address the forecasting of cloud storage capacity consumed using the historic data. This entails the uniqueness and the need of the model developed by the researcher using regression model. The researcher relied more on regression model following the standing views shared by (ORACLE., 2013) that regression is the most popular and reliable method for identifying a linear relationship and forecasting from historical data.

3.0.Methods

Method and source of data collection

The study used secondary data of collected from a private organization. The data was collected using request letter. The letter made a request for a release of the monthly cloud data size (in GB or MB) used for a period of 12 months of 2016.

Sample size

In order to make inference about the population, the sample size used for the analysis was 12 month.

Method of data analysis, procedure and instrument used for analysis

The study used quantitative analysis. The model was based on regression. Minitab18 statistical data analysis software was for model development. In other to develop the forecasting model, the 12 months cloud storage capacity consumed data were keyed into Minitab18 against each corresponding month of consumption. After the model has been developed, the future prediction of cloud storage consumption for each month was made.

The regression model

The regression population model is given by the relation, $Y = \beta 0 + \beta 1 X + \varepsilon.$

The sample (each observation) model relation is given by; $yi = \beta 0 + \beta 1 Xi + \varepsilon i.$

Dependent and Independent Variable

Where **Y** is the dependent variable (cloud storage capacity consumed).

X is the value of the Independent variable (month of cloud storage consumption). It predicts the value of Y. Because the month was used to estimate the change in cloud storage consumption.

β0 is a constant known or the population parameter, (the intercept of the regression line with the Y-axis). It is the value of cloud storage capacity consumption if the value of month equal 0.

β1 is the slope of the regression line, or the population parameter. It tells how much Y (cloud storage capacity consumption) changes for each one-unit change in X (month).

ε is the error term; the error in predicting the value of cloud storage capacity consumption, given the value of the month.

Validation of model

The regression model was validated based on the four assumptions.

I.   **Linearity:** As shown in figure 1 below, the scatterplot indicates a linear relationship between X (month of consumption) and Y (cloud storage capacity consumed). was linear.

Figure 1: Minitab Result Output of Scatterplot for Observation of Linearity between Cloud Storage Capacity Consumed & Period of consumption.

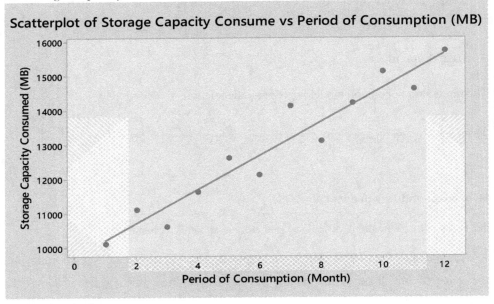

Source: Authors.

II. NORMALITY OF ERRORS: The residuals was approximately normally distributed with the observations near the line as shown at normal probability at figure 2 below. In addition, the P–Value on the normality plot of residual is shown in figure 5 below equals 0.266 > 0.005 at 0.05 level of significance. Hence, the researchers lacked enough to conclude that the data are not normally distributed. Therefore, the null hypothesis (HO) which states that the data are normal was not rejected.

Figure 2: Minitab Result Output of Normality Test.

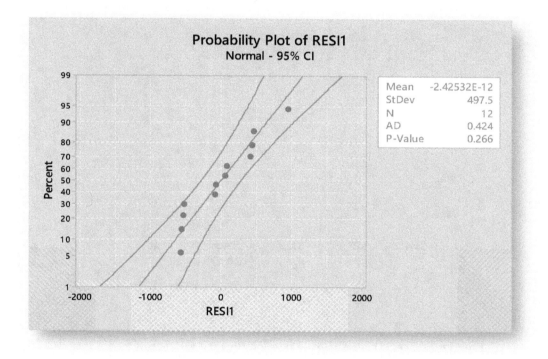

Source: Authors.

III. **INDEPENDENCE OF ERRORS:** There was no relationship between the residuals and the Y variable (cloud storage capacity consumed data). Y was independent of errors, with association approximately 0 (zero). The assumption was met by examining the scatterplot of "residuals versus fits" as shown in figure 3 below.

Figure 3: Minitab Result Output of Scatterplot of Residual versus Fits.

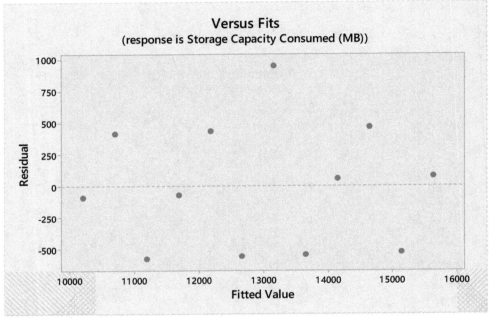

Source: Authors.

IV. **Equal variance.** This assumption demands that the variance of the residuals was the same for all values of X (month of cloud storage capacity consumed). If the plot shows a pattern like bowtie or megaphone shape, then the variances are not consistent. This assumption was met as shown in figure 3 above. The plots are randomly scattered.

Model validation remark: The assumptions for the validation of regression forecasting model was met. The developed model performs well in forecasting.

4.0.Analysis

Regression Equation

Storage Capacity Consumed (MB) = 9702MB + 493.4MB *Month of Consumption

Table 1: Analysis of Variance

Source	DF	Adj SS	Adj MS	F-Value	P-Value
Regression	1	34806311	34806311	127.83	0.000
Period of Consumption (Month)	1	34806311	34806311	127.83	0.000
Error	10	2722855	272286		
Total	11	37529167			

Source: Authors.

Table 2: Model Summary

S	R-sq	R-sq(adj)	R-sq(pred)
521.810	92.74%	92.02%	90.31%

Source: Authors.

Table 3: Coefficients

Term	Coef	SE Coef	T-Value	P-Value	VIF
Constant	9702	321	30.21	0.000	
Period of Consumption (Month)	493.4	43.6	11.31	0.000	1.00

Source: Authors.

Discussion

The P-Value was found to be very low at $0.000 < 0.05$ alpha level of significance. Based on this result the researchers had enough evidence to reject the null hypothesis, which states that $\beta 1 = 0$ (change in cloud storage capacity consumed does not depend on the change in the month of consumption). Since, $\beta 1 \neq 0$, the researcher concluded that change in cloud storage capacity consumed depends on the change in the month of consumption. This simply implies that the cloud storage capacity consumption is associated with the month of consumption. Hence, the month could be used to predict cloud storage consumption.

Remark: While this interpretation seems to reveal causal interpretation. It is noteworthy to clarify that the researchers had no evidence to justify that the increase in the month is causing an increase in cloud storage capacity consumption. In addition, beta values are not enough to justify a causal interpretation.

Key findings

The following three key finding below were made;

- The study revealed that month is a very strong linear predictor of cloud storage capacity consumption.
- Cloud storage capacity consumption either increases or decreases as the month increases.
- Cloud storage service consumers can predict the monthly range or interval of their consumption, irrespective of service provider chosen on GB per month billing.

5.0.Conclusion

The study revealed that change in cloud storage capacity consumed depends on the change in the month of consumption. Hence, the researchers concluded that the month is a globally significant linear predictor of cloud storage capacity consumed at any cloud storage service provider on GB per month billing. The regression model predicts the cloud storage monthly consumption with near accuracy from the actual cloud storage historical. The model determines the cloud storage monthly consumption intervals or ranges for each passing month. Therefore, the month could be relied upon in forecasting cloud storage consumption using regression model.

6.0. References

1. Baughman, McAvoy, McCrory, and O'Connell. (2016, December 9). *Predictive Cloud Computing for professional golf and tennis, Part 8*. Retrieved from IBM: https://www.ibm.com/developerworks/library/ba-predictive-cloud-computing-forecasting-trs/index.html

2. Chandini, Pushpalatha, and Ramesh. (2016). A Brief study on Prediction of load in Cloud Environment. *IJARCCE*, Available on https://www.ijarcce.com/upload/2016/may-16/IJARCCE%2038.pdf.

3. Harvey, C. (2017a). Features & Cost of Popular AWS Services. *Datamation*, Available on https://www.datamation.com/cloud-computing/amazon-web-services.html.

4. Khan, M. R. (2016). *Data Center Load Forecast Using Dependent Mixture Model*. Available on https://openprairie.sdstate.edu/cgi/viewcontent.cgi?article=2120&context=etd.

5. Kondo, D. (2009). *Cost-Benefit Analysis of Cloud Computing versus Desktop Grids*. Available on http://mescal.imag.fr/membres/derrick.kondo/pubs/kondo_hcw09.pdf.

6. Linthicum, D. (2014). The true cost of cloud computing. *Inforworld*, Available on https://www.infoworld.com/article/2841806/cloud-computing/true-cost-cloud-computing.html.

7. Lu, Panneerselvam, Liu and Wu. (2016). RVLBPNN: A Workload Forecasting Model for Smart Cloud Computing. *Scientific Programming*, 9 pages: available on http://dx.doi.org/10.1155/2016/5635673.

8. ORACLE. (2013). *JD Edwards World Forecasting Guide*. Available on https://docs.oracle.com/cd/E26228_01/doc.93/e20706/ap_forcst_calc_ex.htm#WEAFC306.

9. RightScale. (2017). *State od the Cloud Report*. Available on https://assets.rightscale.com/uploads/pdfs/RightScale-2017-State-of-the-Cloud-Report.pdf.

10. Vazquez, Krishnan, and John. (2016). *Time Series Forecasting of Cloud Data Center Workloads*. Available on http://isyou.info/jowua/papers/jowua-v6n3-5.pdf.

11. Yanshuang, Na, Hong, and Yongqiang . (2015). Regression Cloud Models and Their Applications in Energy Consumption of Data Center. *Journal of Electrical and Computer Engineering*, Available on https://www.hindawi.com/journals/jece/2015/143071/.

www.ingramcontent.com/pod-product-compliance
Lightning Source LLC
LaVergne TN
LVHW082125070326
832902LV00041B/2688